MAKE ROOM
FOR GOD

Clearing Life's Clutter
to
Experience More of Jesus

Companion Notebook

TINA RAZZELL

City Walls Press

Table of Contents

About This Book

Welcome to the companion notebook for *Make Room for God, Clearing Life's Clutter to Experience More of Jesus*. This book is filled with reflection questions, journaling prompts, and guided exercises to help you apply each chapter's principles in practical ways.

The questions and actions are the same as in the book, but with room for answers, resolutions, and notes on what you have read.

You might choose to use this book if you are listening to the audio version or reading with an eBook or just don't want to write in the main book.

This journey is about finding freedom, not perfection. Focus on progress and trust God's unique work in your heart and home. Your pace may vary from week to week, but what matters most is continuing to move forward, whether through big changes or small steps. Invite others to join you for encouragement and accountability, as sharing the process makes it easier and more enjoyable. Begin with prayer, asking God to show you what to release and to draw you closer to Him as you make room for what matters most.

Every week, commit to one positive action and build on your progress by adding a new one each week. By the end of the book, you will have eight ways you have resolved to improve your life. No pressure, this is not about perfection. If you succeed in improving your life in one area, that is real progress, and the book has been a success for you. Your resolutions don't need to be different every week. Keep choosing to declutter, or read your Bible more, and you will still be building lasting, positive change.

Chapter 1: Room to Breathe: Meeting God in the Midst of Chaos

Modern life keeps us busy, leaving little room for stillness or connection with God. Our crowded schedules, possessions, and constant demands can drown out His voice and make God feel distant. Deep within, we long for God's presence and the peace that comes from walking closely with Him. By intentionally simplifying our lives, decluttering both our living areas and our minds, we can create room for God to work and focus on what truly matters.

Embracing simplicity in a chaotic world is a spiritual practice. Living with less gives greater clarity about what is truly important. Practical habits such as keeping a box ready for thrift store donations, responsibly disposing of unused items, and shopping mindfully help prevent clutter from returning. Jesus invites us to rest, to step away from chaos and cultivate a quiet, unhurried life so

His presence can dwell. A simplified, intentional life centered on God leads to lasting peace and deeper connection with Him.

DISCUSSION QUESTIONS

1.   What do you do to make time for fellowship with God in your day?

_____

_____

_____

_____

_____

_____

_____

2.   How do you usually get rid of what you no longer need: thrift store, freecycle, person to person giving?

_____

_____

_____

_____

_____

_____

_____

3.   What clutter do you feel is weighing you down and stopping you living the life you were made for?

_____

_____

_____

_____

_____

_____

_____

4.   What would a life of peace and purpose look like for you?

_____

_____

_____

_____

_____

_____

_____

5.   Share about one time you really felt God's presence.

_____

_____

_____

_____

_____

_____

_____

6.   How does busyness or constant distraction in your life affect your ability to experience God's presence, and what small changes could help you create space for Him?

_____

_____

_____

_____

_____

_____

Positive Actions for the Week

Choose an action to commit to this week. If you are doing this study as a group, share with one another which one you are committing to. Or choose an action not from this list that you feel inspired to commit to:

1.   Declutter one room in your house.

2.   Spend 10 minutes a day with God in prayer or Bible reading.

3.   Don't buy anything new (except food or consumables).

4.   Start a designated box for items to donate, add at least one thing to it daily. Commit to donating it in a month's time.

5.   Choose a place in your home that will become a place for you to pray.

6.   Choose one hour this week to rest intentionally. No chores, no work, no screens, just worship, journaling, or sitting in silence before God.

What positive action are you committing to this week?

1. _____

_____

_____

_____

JOURNAL TIME (for your eyes only)

What have you learned from this week's chapter?

_____

_____

_____

_____

_____

_____

_____

_____

_____

_____

_____

_____

_____

_____

_____

_____

_____

Chapter 2: Declutter Your Home: Inviting God into Your Living Space

Aligning your space with your faith begins with embracing simplicity over excess. True peace doesn't come from adding more, but from creating a home that reflects God's presence and priorities. Jesus' teachings remind us to trust God, live free from materialism, and focus on eternal treasures rather than earthly possessions. When our homes and hearts are cluttered, whether by stuff, digital noise, or overpacked schedules, it becomes harder to experience peace or hear God's voice. By simplifying, we open space for His presence and create an environment that nurtures rest, gratitude, and spiritual growth.

Decluttering is more than just a task, it is a spiritual practice. Small, consistent habits like 15-30 minute sessions or using the Three-Box Method can bring meaningful change over time. Practicing mindful consumption through "one in, one out" and waiting before buying helps prevent clutter from returning. Letting go of sentimental items is an act of trust, remembering that memories reside in our hearts, not in things. As we release what no longer serves us, we make room for sacred spaces where we can encounter God's peace. Simplifying our surroundings ultimately leads to spiritual freedom, clearing away distractions so we can live fully in His presence.

DISCUSSION QUESTIONS

1.   What are the most cluttered areas in your home, and why do you think they accumulate so much stuff?

_____

_____

_____

_____

_____

_____

_____

2.   How can we let go of what we don't need and trust God over material possessions?

_____

_____

_____

_____

_____

_____

_____

3.   How can we intentionally create space for God in our living environment?

_____

_____

_____

_____

_____

_____

4.   What strategies, such as the Three-Box Method, have you found most effective for decluttering?

_____

_____

_____

_____

_____

_____

_____

5.　　How do you decide what to keep and what
to part with?

_____

_____

_____

_____

_____

_____

_____

6.　　How could simplifying your home impact
your peace and connection with God?

_____

_____

_____

_____

_____

_____

_____

Positive Actions for the Week

Choose an action to commit to this week. If you are doing this study as a group, share with one another which one you are committing to. Or choose an action not from this list that you feel inspired to commit to:

1.   Look at your kitchen and see how it can be simplified.

2.   Dedicate 15 minutes a day to using the "give-away, throw away, put away" method.

3.   Reduce clothing or shoes in your closet.

4.   Choose a Psalm, or one Bible verse and meditate on it daily.

5.   Research a non-profit you can give your time to.

6.   Write down, rather than buy, anything you feel tempted to purchase this week. Revisit the list after seven days and see if you still want those items.

What positive action are you committing to this week?

Copy the positive actions from last week and place this week's resolve at number 2.

1. _____

_____

_____

_____

2. _____

_____

_____

_____

JOURNAL TIME (for your eyes only)

What have you learned from this week's chapter?

_____

_____

_____

_____

_____

_____

_____

_____

_____

_____

_____

_____

_____

_____

_____

_____

_____

_____

_____

Chapter 3: The Art of Intentional Living: Creating Space for Peace

Bring the "hotel feeling" home by creating a light, restful, and inviting environment in your home through simplifying as much as you can. Regularly declutter your home and your time, keeping only what you love, use, and truly need. Simplify your schedule by removing nonessential commitments and make space for what matters most.

Practice daily gratitude to shift your focus from restlessness to contentment and prioritize rest in every form to restore balance and avoid burnout. Set healthy boundaries that protect your time for rest and self-care, and extend hospitality through simplicity, welcoming others into your home even when it's not perfect. Above all, live intentionally, aligning your values, goals, and routines with God's purpose so that your days reflect both meaningful productivity and sacred rest.

DISCUSSION QUESTIONS

1.   Which of these practices (decluttering, gratitude, rest, boundaries, hospitality, intentional living) feels most challenging for you, and why?

_____

_____

_____

_____

_____

_____

_____

2.   What small changes have you made in your home to create a more relaxing and clutter-free environment?

_____

_____

_____

_____

_____

_____

_____

3.   What personal boundaries could you have
to protect your own well-being?

_____

_____

_____

_____

_____

_____

4.   In what ways do you incorporate stillness,
prayer, or reflection into your daily routine?

_____

_____

_____

_____

_____

_____

5.   How could you bring even a little of the
hotel atmosphere into your home?

_____

_____

_____

_____

_____

_____

_____

6.　How might simplifying your schedule and commitments create more space for rest and meaningful relationships?

_____

_____

_____

_____

Positive Actions for the Week

Choose an action to commit to this week. If you are doing this study as a group, share with one another which one you are committing to. Or choose an action not from this list that you feel inspired to commit to:

1.　Look at your bedroom and see how it can be simplified.

2. Observe Sabbath this week or plan to do nothing for a period of each day.

3. Go for a walk in nature, enjoy God's creation.

4. Spend 15 minutes a day with God in prayer and Bible reading.

5. Each day this week, write down three things you are grateful for. Focus on small, ordinary blessings and thank God for each one.

6.   Go on a date with your significant other, or a close friend.

What positive action are you committing to this week?

Copy the positive actions from previous weeks and place this week's resolve at number 3.

1. _____

_____

_____

_____

2. _____

_____

_____

_____

3. _____

_____

_____

_____

JOURNAL TIME (for your eyes only)

What have you learned from this week's chapter?

_____

_____

_____

_____

_____

_____

_____

_____

_____

_____

_____

_____

_____

_____

_____

_____

_____

_____

Chapter 4: Simplify Your Online Life: Strategies to Reduce Binge-Watching and Scrolling

Technology is a powerful tool, but when it dominates our attention, it can isolate us from real-life connection. To recover the art of being present, we must recognize how screens and endless scrolling pull us away from the world God placed before us. Reflect on your priorities by examining how your screen time aligns with your values. Technology should serve you, not control you. Protect your relationships by choosing real conversations over virtual ones, since true fellowship happens face-to-face.

Set clear boundaries around your digital habits: limit social media, create tech-free zones or times, and silence devices when with others. Practice digital fasting and weekly "screen Sabbaths" to rest your mind and draw closer to God through prayer and stillness. Replace screen time with creative, hands-on activities to rediscover the joy of simple pleasures. Be intentional and accountable. Plan your online use thoughtfully and invite trusted friends to help you stay mindful. Wise, consistent choices lead to deeper peace, stronger relationships, and a richer connection with God.

DISCUSSION QUESTIONS

1.   How do smartphones and constant connectivity affect your ability to experience simple, real-world moments?

_____

_____

_____

_____

_____

_____

_____

2.   How could small changes, such as limiting notifications or avoiding phones in the morning, improve your productivity and well-being?

_____

_____

_____

_____

_____

_____

_____

3.   Have you ever gone on a digital fast? How did you fare?

_____

_____

_____

_____

_____

4.   When was the last time you felt ignored or disconnected because of someone's phone use?

_____

_____

_____

_____

_____

_____

5.   Do you feel in control of your device usage, or does it sometimes feel like it controls you?

_____

_____

_____

_____

_____

_____

6.   What would you do if you reduced your screen time?

_____

_____

_____

_____

_____

_____

Positive Actions for the Week

Choose an action to commit to this week. If you are doing this study as a group, share with one another which one you are committing to. Or choose an action not from this list that you feel inspired to commit to:

1. Declutter your bathroom cupboards.

2. Examine the apps on your phone and delete some.

3. Plan a hobby that doesn't involve screens.

4. Delay looking at any screens for the first 30 minutes after waking.

5.   Choose a time each evening to turn off your phone and screens.

6.   Commit to one meal this week where all devices are turned off.

What positive action are you committing to this week?

Copy the positive actions from previous weeks and place this week's resolve at number 4.

1. _____
_____
_____
_____

2. _____
_____
_____
_____

3. _____
_____
_____
_____

4. _____
_____
_____
_____

JOURNAL TIME (for your eyes only)

What have you learned from this week's chapter?

_____

_____

_____

_____

_____

_____

_____

_____

_____

_____

_____

_____

_____

_____

_____

_____

_____

_____

_____

Chapter 5: Doing Less, Doing Better: Heavenly Focused, Sabbath Rest.

In a world that glorifies busyness, choosing to slow down is a spiritual act of resistance, creating space for peace and God's presence. As parents, we can model a God-centered life by simplifying our schedules, prioritizing meaningful conversations, and cherishing quality time together. Like Mary at Jesus' feet, we are called to choose presence over perfection, valuing relationships above performance. Observing the Sabbath offers a sacred rhythm of rest and renewal, inviting us to pause, worship, and reconnect with God and loved ones. By building margin into our days, we prevent burnout and make room to discern God's will. Committing every decision to Him helps us practice His presence throughout the day. Setting healthy boundaries and learning to say no preserves our time and energy for what truly matters. Ultimately, doing fewer things with excellence and intention allows us to discover the deep joy and freedom found in a simple life that glorifies God.

DISCUSSION QUESTIONS

1.   How does the practice of intentionally slowing down, such as taking the longest line at the supermarket, challenge our modern pace of life?

_____

_____

_____

_____

_____

_____

_____

2.   Many people feel pressured to enroll their children in multiple activities. How can parents balance structured learning with unstructured, creative time for their children?

_____

_____

_____

_____

_____

_____

_____

3.   In the story of Mary and Martha, which character do you relate to more? How can you balance the need to "do" with the need to "be" in your own life?

_____

_____

_____

_____

_____

_____

4.   How can you cultivate a deeper sense of God's presence in your everyday life, while also simplifying your schedule to focus on what truly matters?

_____

_____

_____

_____

_____

_____

_____

5.   Have you ever practiced a Sabbath? Share your experiences.

_____

_____

_____

_____

_____

_____

6.   How would your life change if every decision was surrendered to God?

_____

_____

_____

_____

_____

_____

Positive Actions for the Week

Choose an action to commit to this week. If you are doing this study as a group, share with one

another which one you are committing to. Or choose an action not from this list that you feel inspired to commit to:

1.   Declutter your paperwork pile

2.   Make a conscious effort to include God in every decision throughout your day.

3.   Set aside a specific time each week to disconnect from work and busyness to refocus on faith and family.

4.   Start or end each day by writing down three things you are grateful for.

5.   Commit to reading and meditating on a Bible passage each day.

6.   Write down 50–100 things you are thankful for, big or small. Read it out loud as a prayer of gratitude.

What positive action are you committing to this week?

Copy the positive actions from previous weeks and place this week's resolve at number 5.

1. _____
_____
_____

2. _____
_____
_____

3. _____
_____
_____

4. _____
_____
_____

5. _____
_____
_____

JOURNAL TIME (for your eyes only)

What have you learned from this week's chapter?

_____

_____

_____

_____

_____

_____

_____

_____

_____

_____

_____

_____

_____

_____

_____

_____

_____

_____

Chapter 6: Investing in Time with Jesus: Prayer, Worship, and the Word

Deep engagement with Scripture keeps God's Word alive and meaningful. Establishing consistent rhythms of prayer and Bible reading, setting a consistent time and place, and memorizing verses help build lasting spiritual habits. Scripture hidden in our hearts allows the Holy Spirit to bring truth and encouragement when we need it most. Prayer is not about performance but relationship, an ongoing conversation with Jesus that includes both speaking and listening. Journaling and meditating on Scripture help quiet our hearts to hear His voice.

Worship, too, is more than music. It is a lifestyle of devotion and obedience to God's heart. Sacred moments with Him can happen in ordinary tasks when we remain aware of His presence. Preparing our hearts for corporate worship and tending to our own well-being remove barriers that keep us from fully engaging with Him. True worship involves our whole selves: body, mind, and spirit, offered in love to the One who is worthy.

DISCUSSION QUESTIONS

1.   How do you incorporate prayer and Bible reading into your daily routine, even during a busy day?

_____

_____

_____

_____

_____

_____

2.   What role does gratitude play in your prayer life?

_____

_____

_____

_____

_____

_____

3.　　What distractions or struggles prevent you from fully engaging in prayer or worship?

_____

_____

_____

_____

_____

_____

4.　　How do you personally connect with God in worship outside of a church setting?

_____

_____

_____

_____

_____

_____

5.　　How do you currently engage with Scripture? By reading, listening, journaling, studying, or something else?

_____

_____

_____

_____

_____

_____

_____

6.   Have you ever taken intentional time to be silent and simply listen for God's voice? What has that experience been like for you?

_____

_____

_____

_____

_____

_____

Positive Actions for the Week

Choose an action to commit to this week. If you are doing this study as a group, share with one another which one you are committing to. Or choose an action not from this list that you feel inspired to commit to:

1. Look at your family room and see how it can be simplified.

2. Find and start a regular Bible reading plan.

3. Pray aloud in a small group or go on a prayer walk.

4. Take time to worship this week.

5. Choose one verse to memorize.

6.   Spend 5 minutes in silence each day, inviting God to speak.

GROUP CHALLENGE

If you are studying as a group, designate a portion of your meeting time to practice different forms of prayer and worship together. You could try:

1.   Read a Psalm together and discuss how it inspires worship.

2.   Sharing a favorite worship song and what it means to you.

3.   Taking turns leading a short prayer or sharing a personal prayer request.

4.   Practicing silence as a form of prayer, then sharing what God revealed in that time.

5.   Provide time for everyone to write prayers in a journal, then allow volunteers to share parts if they feel comfortable.

6.   Encourage members to express worship through art, poetry, or movement, reflecting on how their creativity connects them to God.

7.   Pair members up for short, focused prayer sessions, then rotate partners so everyone experiences different perspectives and prayers.

8. Take turns naming things you're thankful for and conclude with a collective prayer of thanksgiving.

What positive action are you committing to this week?

Copy the positive actions from previous weeks and place this week's resolve at number 6.

1. _____
   _____

2. _____
   _____

3. _____
   _____

4. _____
   _____

5. _____
   _____

6. _____
   _____

JOURNAL TIME (for your eyes only)

What have you learned from this week's chapter?

_____

_____

_____

_____

_____

_____

_____

_____

_____

_____

_____

_____

_____

_____

_____

_____

_____

_____

Chapter 7: Buying Wisely: Generosity and Contentment

Redefining simplicity begins with mindful choices, even in something as personal as clothing. After losing weight, the author chose a minimalist wardrobe as a reflection of a simpler, more intentional lifestyle. Recognizing the pull of overconsumption and online marketing helps break the cycle of impulsive spending and cultivates gratitude for what we already have. True contentment is found not in possessions but in trusting God's provision.

Practical simplicity means setting healthy boundaries: making thoughtful purchase lists, waiting before buying, budgeting wisely, and keeping a smaller, intentional wardrobe. Choosing quality over quantity supports both sustainability and ethical living. Clothing should meet needs modestly and purposefully, without becoming a source of pride or identity. Generosity then becomes a natural expression of simplicity: giving time and resources freely. Ultimately, living simply allows us to live for Jesus, not for stuff, focusing our hearts on what truly matters: His Kingdom.

DISCUSSION QUESTIONS

1.   How does our culture's focus on consumerism and abundance contrast with the Biblical call to simplicity and contentment?

_____

_____

_____

_____

_____

_____

_____

2.   Have you experienced the pressure of marketing or "fear of missing out" when it comes to making purchases?

_____

_____

_____

_____

_____

_____

_____

3.   How can practices like budgeting, decluttering, or waiting before purchases help us align our habits with God's principles?

_____

_____

_____

_____

_____

_____

4.   What does generosity mean to you personally, and how can you practice it in everyday life?

_____

_____

_____

_____

_____

_____

5. Does your current wardrobe, home, and lifestyle reflect your deepest values?

_____

_____

_____

_____

_____

_____

6. The chapter challenges us to support ethical businesses and reduce overconsumption. How do we balance affordability, convenience, and our values when we shop?

_____

_____

_____

_____

_____

_____

Positive Actions for the Week

Choose an action to commit to this week. If you are doing this study as a group, share with one

another which one you are committing to. Or choose an action not from this list that you feel inspired to commit to:

1.   Go in your closet and remove items you no longer use, selling or donating what is still useful.

2.   Before making any non-essential purchase, wait at least 24 hours to consider if it truly adds value.

3.   Rotate between just a few outfits for one week to practice simplicity in your wardrobe.

4.   Perform one act of generosity this week without expecting anything in return.

5.   Unsubscribe from marketing emails or block targeted ads to reduce consumer temptations.

6.   Research one product you regularly buy (clothes, coffee, shoes, etc.). Find out where it comes from and whether the workers are paid fairly. Consider switching to a more ethical option if possible.

What positive action are you committing to this week?

Copy the positive actions from previous weeks and place this week's resolve at number 7.

1. _____
_____

2. _____
_____

3. _____
_____

4. _____
_____

5. _____
_____

6. _____
_____

7. _____
_____

JOURNAL TIME (for your eyes only)

What have you learned from this week's chapter?

_____

_____

_____

_____

_____

_____

_____

_____

_____

_____

_____

_____

_____

_____

_____

_____

_____

_____

Chapter 8: Loving God, Loving Others: Nurturing Connection for an Abundant Life

A strong relationship with God is the foundation of a meaningful life. Time spent in Scripture, prayer, and worship keeps us centered on Him, even as different seasons of life bring new challenges and rhythms. Each stage, whether busy or quiet, carries purpose and deepens our spiritual growth. As we let go of possessions, distractions, and mental clutter, we make room for God to move more freely in our hearts and lives.

Love, like faith, is a daily choice. Healthy relationships grow through intentional acts of kindness and sacrifice. True community takes time and a willingness to serve one another. When we simplify our lives, we create space for the fruits of the Spirit to grow. True abundance is found in Christ alone, living "joined to the Vine," trusting His provision, and embracing a life of peace, joy, and purpose.

DISCUSSION QUESTIONS

1.   How can practices like budgeting, decluttering, or waiting before purchases help us align our habits with God's principles?

_____

_____

_____

_____

_____

_____

2.   What are some habits, or attitudes in your life that might need to be "pruned" so you can grow in love and peace?

_____

_____

_____

_____

_____

_____

_____

3.   The author talks about sharing meals daily as a way to build connection. What is one practical way you could be more intentional about connecting with your family, friends, or church community?

_____

_____

_____

_____

_____

_____

4.   How does your relationship with God influence the way you interact with others in your daily life?

_____

_____

_____

_____

_____

_____

5. In what ways can letting go of distractions or mental clutter help you cultivate healthier relationships?

_____

_____

_____

_____

_____

_____

_____

6. How can you intentionally practice love and kindness in relationships, even when it feels inconvenient or challenging?

_____

_____

_____

_____

_____

_____

Positive Actions for the Week

Choose an action to commit to this week. If you are doing this study as a group, share with one

another which one you are committing to. Or choose an action not from this list that you feel inspired to commit to:

1.   Choose a drawer, closet, or room and remove items you no longer use, donating what is still useful.

2.   Before making any non-essential purchase, wait at least 24 hours to consider if it truly adds value.

3.   Each day, write down three things you are thankful for.

4.   Perform one act of generosity this week without expecting anything in return.

5.   Set aside one block of time to slow down, worship, rest, and spend time with God, creating space for Him to refresh your spirit.

6.   Choose one evening to put phones and screens away and spend that time connecting with family, sharing a meal, or having a meaningful conversation.

Write all the positive actions you have committed to.

1. _____
_____

2. _____
_____

3. _____
_____

4. _____
_____

5. _____
_____

6. _____
_____

7. _____
_____

8. _____
_____

JOURNAL TIME (for your eyes only)

What have you learned from this book?

_____

_____

_____

_____

_____

_____

_____

_____

_____

_____

_____

_____

_____

_____

_____

_____

_____

_____

And Finally

If you have improved your life in one way, the book has been a success. Even if you haven't improved, I hope you have at least seen your possessions in a new light and realized there are so many more important things.

Turn your eyes upon Jesus

Look full in His wonderful face

And the things of earth will grow strangely dim

In the light of His glory and grace

- Helen Howarth Lemmel